Witch Hazel gets Married

E. Larreula R. Capdevila
A. Wilkinson

Cambridge University Press
Cambridge   New York   Port Chester
Melbourne   Sydney

I could feel something special in the air that spring morning. 'Witch Hazel,' I said to myself in the mirror, 'You're a rare sight! Still so young and beautiful!'
'You look just the same to me as you did yesterday,' muttered Goggletoot.
Now Goggletoot is my dearest friend, but owls never can see clearly in the daylight, can they?

Anyway, as I was sweeping up, I had a very good idea.
'Goggletoot,' I said. 'It's high time I got married.
I must start looking for a husband at once!'
Just then, I saw something glinting on the floor.
It was a gold coin.
'Come on, Goggletoot, this is just what we need!'

First of all I advertised for a husband in the Ghoul's
Gazette. Then Goggletoot and I took off on my
zoom-broom and flew straight to the draper's shop to buy
some ribbon. I needed to look my very best.
At last I found the perfect thing – a sky-blue ribbon with
blue moons dotted all over it. Goggletoot had the same idea.

We sped home to try on our new ribbons. I
thought Goggletoot's ribbon was a bit bright, but
I didn't want to hurt his feelings so I kept quiet.
But I was delighted with how smart *I* looked.

'A wife for you, a husband for me,
  We'll soon be married, just wait and see!'
I trilled to Goggletoot. But Goggletoot was not
so sure about finding a wife.

I was in such a good mood that I decided it was
time to give my house a grand spring-clean. I do
like to see a few pretty spider's webs around the
house, but really, these spiders were beginning to
get a bit too cheeky.

I started with the dirty glass in the front door.
After all, it's no good looking beautiful if no-one
can see in, is it? No sooner had I got up a brilliant
shine, when who should jog past but Roddy
Rattlebones. When he saw me, he came to a
clattering stop and asked me to marry him!

'I'm sorry, Roddy, but I can't marry you,' I told him. 'I can't have you and your bones rattling all over my house. The noise would give me a headache.' Poor Roddy Rattlebones was very disappointed. I never knew skeletons could cry, did you?

Meanwhile Goggletoot had been courting a fluffy white hen but she wasn't impressed.

She gave him a pumpkin to make up for saying no.

A little later, I was busy mopping the floor of
my broom garage when I heard a polite cough
behind me. It was Frank Frankenstein, the monster from
the castle on the next hill.
'Hrrumph, hrrumph . . . Excuse me, Witch Hazel, you're
looking perfectly charming today. Would you like to marry me?'

'I'm sorry, Frank, but I can't marry you. I would be forever tripping over your big feet and I could never afford to buy all the toothpaste you need to clean those teeth of yours.'
Mind you, I thought he looked rather handsome in his spotted pink tie.

Goggletoot had taken a shine to a goggle-eyed frog.
But *she* gave him a pumpkin too.

My next job was vacuuming the carpets. I was doing very well when suddenly the vacuum cleaner started to make a strange moaning sound 'HOOOOOOOHH!' When I looked up I saw that the sound wasn't coming from the vacuum cleaner at all but from a ghost standing in the middle of my hall in his underpants.

He asked if I wouldn't mind giving him back
his sheet as he was getting chilly.
'By the way,' he added, 'you do look nice.
Will you marry me?'
I was trying my hardest not to laugh.
'I'm sorry, but I can't marry you. It would take
me all day washing and ironing those underpants
of yours, not to mention your sheet!'

Goggletoot's latest love was a charming little caterpillar,
but oh dear, along came another pumpkin!

It was time for some carpet beating up on the battlements. I was in full swing when I saw a large bat swooping down towards me. As I raised my beater to chase him off, he called out, 'My dear Madam Hazel, it is I, Count Batula! I have heard that you're looking for a husband. Look no further! You'll find none smarter than me.' I chased him off at once. 'You may be smart,' I shouted after him, 'but I know all about you bats. You sleep all day and you're out all night!'

But a bat wife would have quite suited Goggletoot. Alas it was not to be . . .

A little later, I was up in the tower clearing
the cobwebs. I was beginning to feel rather
fed up. So was Goggletoot. He didn't even
like pumpkins! Then I heard a mumbling
sound coming from below. 'Mmmmmm . . .
mmm . . . mmm!' It was a mummy – not at all
like *your* mummy, of course – but the sort
which is all nicely wrapped up. I think he was
asking me to marry him but I couldn't hear a
word he was saying. And what good is a
husband if you can't have a decent chat once
in a while?

Goggletoot thought that a spider-wife would
be able to spin him a tale from time to time,
but this spider wouldn't . . .

As you know, we witches like night-time best, so I said to Goggletoot, 'Come on, Goggletoot, let's get out into the night air and sweep up the dead leaves.' Very soon, I heard a shuffling and a crackling of leaves nearby.

A wolf-man came out from among the trees.
'Please marry me, Witch Hazel!' he said, smacking
his lips together a mite too eagerly for my taste.
'No, thank you,' I told him firmly. 'If you can't
decide whether you're a man or a wolf, then I won't
know either. And I certainly can't marry both of you.'
He loped off into the forest, howling.

Next I got down to the washing. It was nearly dawn when I hung it out to dry.
'I'm afraid it's time for bed now, Goggletoot,' I said sadly. 'We didn't have much luck finding a mate, did we?'

I had hardly finished saying these words when out of the blue appeared the most handsome wizard I had ever seen! I fell in love with him at once!

His crow wasn't bad-looking either. Goggletoot fell in love with *her* in a flash. It was the real thing!

My wizard said his name was Wilko, and that
he had fallen head-over-heels in love with me
– so much so, that he had quite a bruise under
his hat. He gave me a beautiful cactus and
asked me to marry him.
'Yes,' I said. 'I would love to marry you.'

We decided that the wedding should be the
very next night. So we spent that morning
sending out invitations to all our friends by
pigeon post. Goggletoot and Cathy Crow, who
wanted to get married too, had the same idea,
though I was a little doubtful if *their* postman
was up to the job.

So, we got married. Our friends showered us with magic dust as we flew to our special wedding feast on the highest mountain in the land.
My feet were in the clouds and my head felt dizzy, I was so happy!

We had a delicious feast and Wilko
told us some funny stories about some
of his magic spells which had gone
wrong. There were quite a few . . .
Then he opened the champagne and
filled our glasses.
We were about to drink to a long and
happy marriage when a terrible thing
happened.

No sooner had a drop of champagne passed
Wilko's lips than he started to shrink . . . and
shrink . . . and shrink . . . until he vanished
altogether! Horror of horrors – my beloved
husband had disappeared. And Goggletoot's
beloved Cathy had disappeared too!
We threw down our full glasses at once!
'Wilko must have uncorked a bottle of his
vanishing potion by mistake!' I shrieked.

Goggletoot and I were heartbroken. Day and night we watched out for them. But there was no sign of them in the sky and no news of them in the newspaper.
No magic in the world – not even mine – could ever bring them back. But I was sure of one thing. No other husband would do.

Published by the Press Syndicate of the University of Cambridge
The Pitt Building, Trumpington Street, Cambridge CB2 1RP
40 West 20th Street, New York, NY 10011, USA
10 Stamford Road, Oakleigh, Melbourne 3166, Australia

Originally published in Spanish 1987 as *La Boda de la Bruja Aburrida*
by Editorial Ariel S.A., Barcelona
© 1987 Editorial Ariel S.A.
First published in English by Cambridge University Press 1989 as *Witch Hazel gets Married*.
English edition © Cambridge University Press 1989

Printed in Spain

British Library cataloguing-in-publication data
Larreula, E.
Witch Hazel gets Married.
I. Title II. Capdevila, R. III. Wilkinson, A.
IV. La Boda de la Bruja Aburrida. *English*
863′.64 [J]

ISBN 0 521 37357 3